PROFESSOR HOOT'S SCIENCE COMICS

SPACE

WRITTEN BY MINERVA BLACK
ILLUSTRATED BY RICHARD WATSON

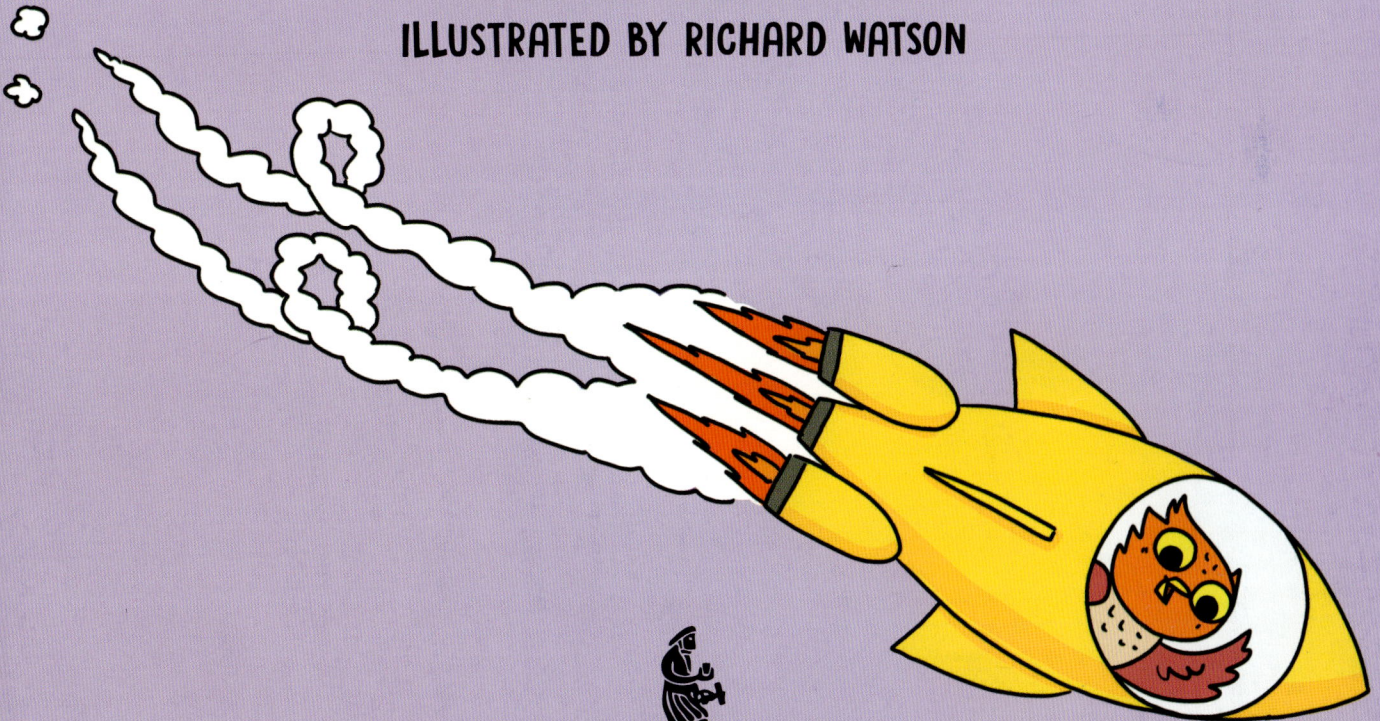

WAYLAND

First published in Great Britain in 2025 by Wayland
Copyright © Hodder and Stoughton, 2025

Wayland, an imprint of
Hachette Children's Group
Part of Hodder and Stoughton
Carmelite House
50 Victoria Embankment
London EC4Y 0DZ

An Hachette UK Company
www.hachette.co.uk
www.hachettechildrens.co.uk

HB ISBN: 978 1 5263 2781 9
PB ISBN: 978 1 5263 2783 3
ebook ISBN: 978 1 5263 2782 6

Illustration: Richard Watson
Commissioning editor: Jenni Lazell

Printed in China

FSC
www.fsc.org
MIX
Paper | Supporting
responsible forestry
FSC® C104740

The authorised representative in the EEA is Hachette Ireland,
8 Castlecourt Centre, Dublin 15, D15 XTP3, Ireland
(email: info@hbgi.ie)

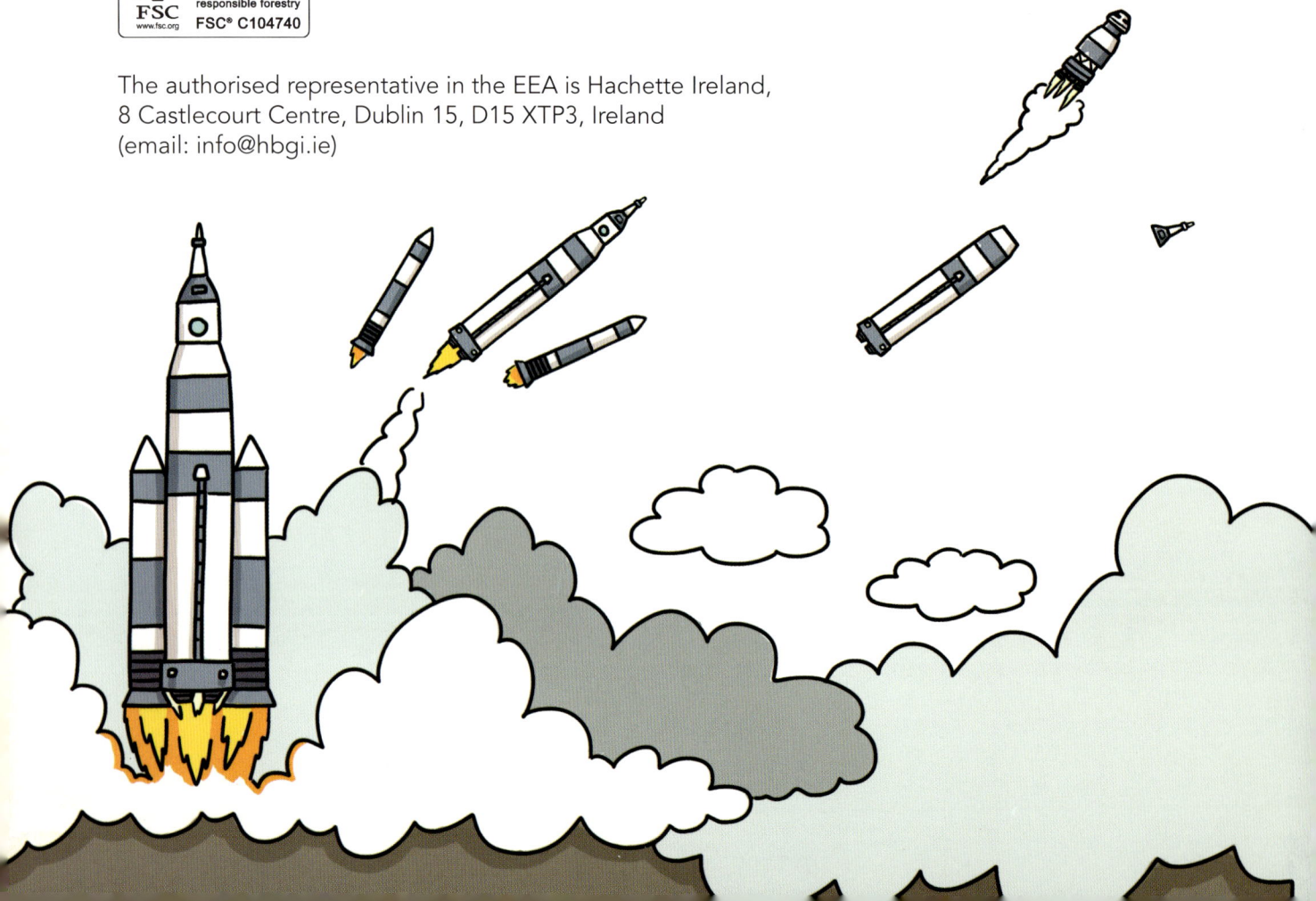

PROFESSOR HOOT'S SCIENCE COMICS

SPACE

WRITTEN BY MINERVA BLACK
ILLUSTRATED BY RICHARD WATSON

CONTENTS

Professor Hoot flies off in search of a learning adventure to bring back to the Night School for Wise Young Owls.

To us, Earth seems to be an enormous place. But it's just a small member of a whole group of planets. Earth is probably the only place in our Solar System where there is life.

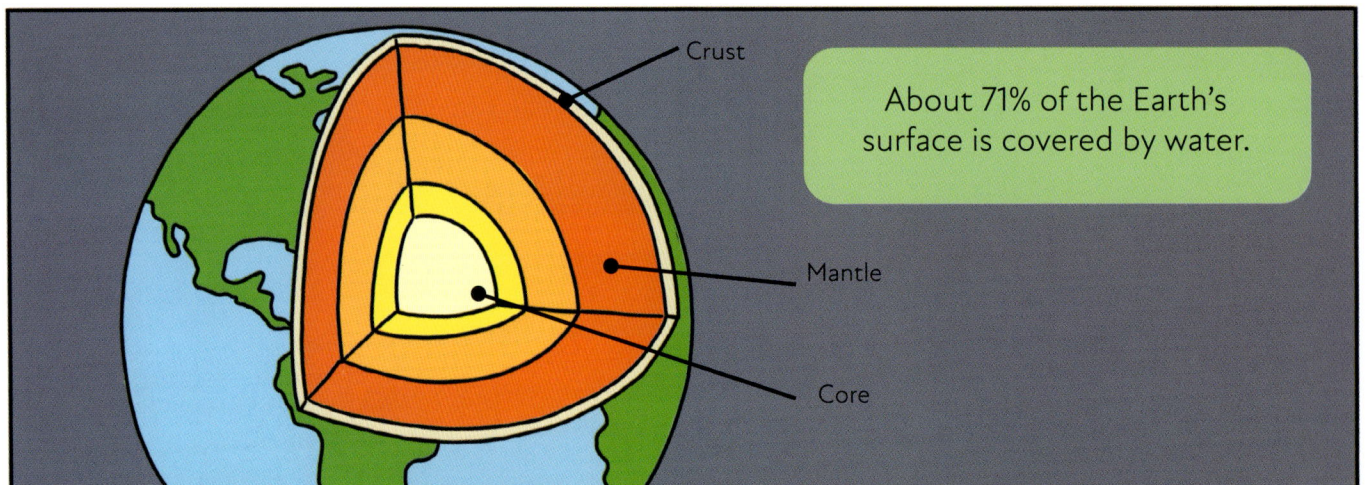

Here I go!

Wow – is that Earth? It's so beautiful.

Crust

Mantle

Core

About 71% of the Earth's surface is covered by water.

Earth is a giant ball of hot rock made of three main layers. Earth's blue oceans and green vegetation make it look very different to other planets. We know it as the 'Blue Planet.'

The Moon is Earth's only natural satellite (an object that orbits, or circles, another object). It is about a quarter of the size of Earth.

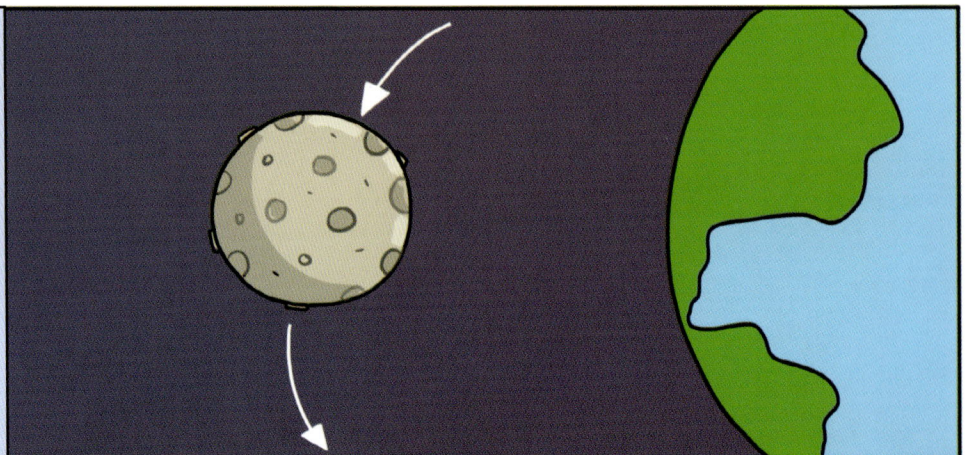

The Moon looks very different to Earth. Its surface is covered with craters, rocks and powdery dust and pebbles.

That's one giant leap for owlkind!

Because the Moon is smaller than Earth, the effect of gravity is weaker. You can jump six times further on the Moon!

Astronauts first landed on the Moon on 20 July, 1969. They walked on its surface and carried out several experiments. Because there is no wind, their footprints are still there.

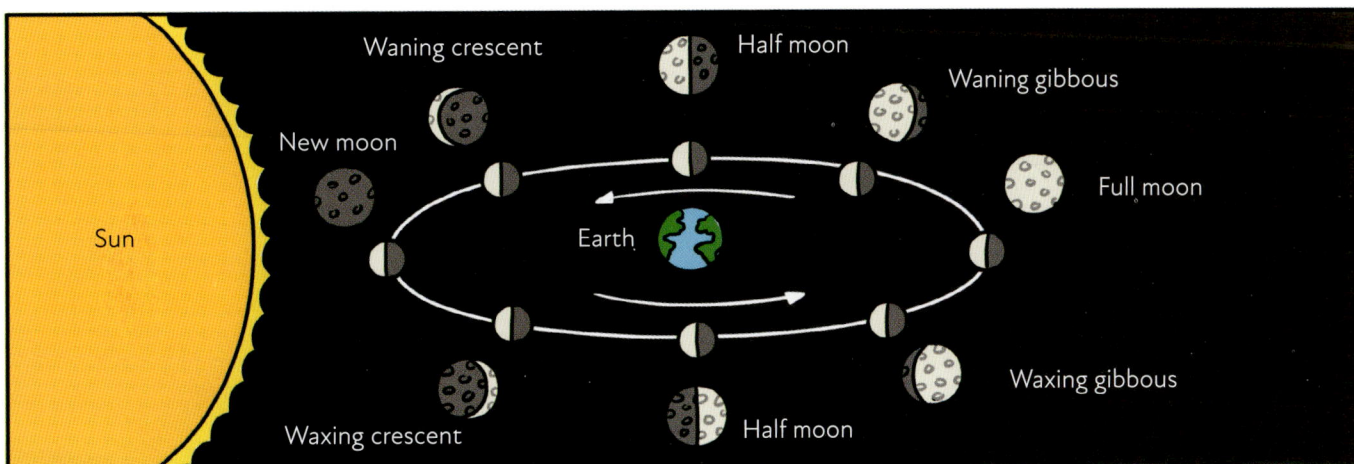

Waning crescent

Half moon

Waning gibbous

New moon

Sun

Earth

Full moon

Waxing crescent

Half moon

Waxing gibbous

We see the Moon from Earth because light from the Sun bounces off it. The Sun lights only one side. The Moon seems to change shape from day to day because we see different parts of this lit side as the Moon moves around its orbit.

People have always dreamed of leaving Earth but the technology didn't exist until the 1950s, when the USA and the Soviet Union were competing in a race to space.

The Soviet Union led the way, launching the first satellite, called *Sputnik*, into orbit around Earth in 1957.

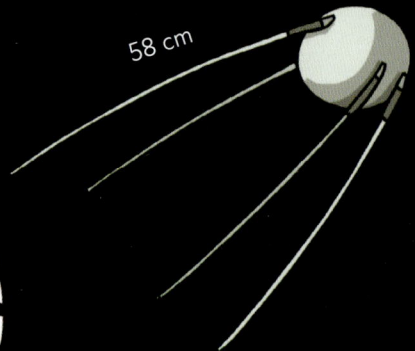
58 cm

Four radio antennae

Woof?

Later that year, *Sputnik 2* carried the dog Laika into orbit. Sadly, she didn't return to Earth.

In 1961, Yuri Gagarin in the space capsule *Vostok 1* was the first human in space.

Lunar module

Command and service module

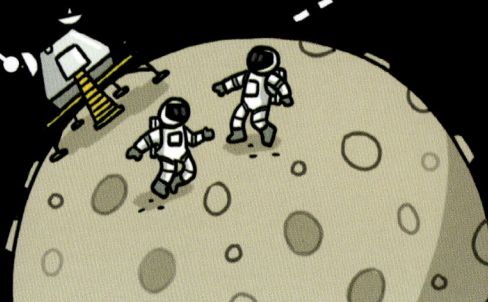

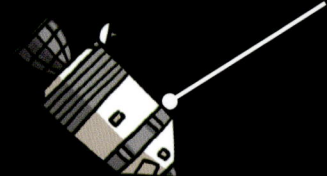

The space race concluded with the 1969 US Apollo 11 mission, when two astronauts, Neil Armstrong and Buzz Aldrin, landed on the Moon while a third, Michael Collins, waited in orbit.

We have lift off!

2 - Booster rockets drop away.

1 - Lift off

3 - Main fuel tank drops away.

It takes a lot of power to launch a rocket. The main part of a rocket is a long tube filled with fuel. As the fuel burns, it pushes gas downwards, which pushes the rocket up. Then the empty fuel tanks drop away.

Building the International Space Station was the joint effort of 15 countries. It has been occupied since the year 2000 and continues to be a place for scientific research.

Potential astronauts have to study very hard to go to space. They train underwater as it's like being in microgravity.

So how did Earth, the Moon and all the other things in space come to be?
For this explanation we need to go back in time ... 13.7 billion years!

I knew this time-travel feature would come in handy.

13.8 billion years ago, the Universe exploded out of a single point at a moment we call the Big Bang. But it didn't actually make that loud a sound.

Over billions of years, atoms and molecules formed, as well as clouds of space dust, stars and galaxies. 4.6 billion years ago, a very special star formed – the Sun!

The centre of the Sun is about 15 MILLION °C.

Aren't you bright!

Aww, Earth is just a baby planet. Well I'd better get back home to the present.

Not long after that (about 60 million years) the Earth formed, though it looked very different to how it does today. For millions of years, it was filled with volcanoes and gas clouds.

Galaxies are vast regions of stars, gas, dust and other space objects grouped together, and surrounded by empty space. A single galaxy contains millions of stars and there are millions of galaxies.

YOU ARE HERE.

Our Solar System is in a galaxy called the Milky Way. It's called this because you can see it in Earth's night sky as a faint band of light.

There are over 100 billion stars in the Milky Way.

Our Solar System consists of the Sun, the eight planets that orbit it, the moons of these planets and many other objects that are affected by the Sun's gravity. It is gravity that keeps every planet circling, or orbiting, the Sun.

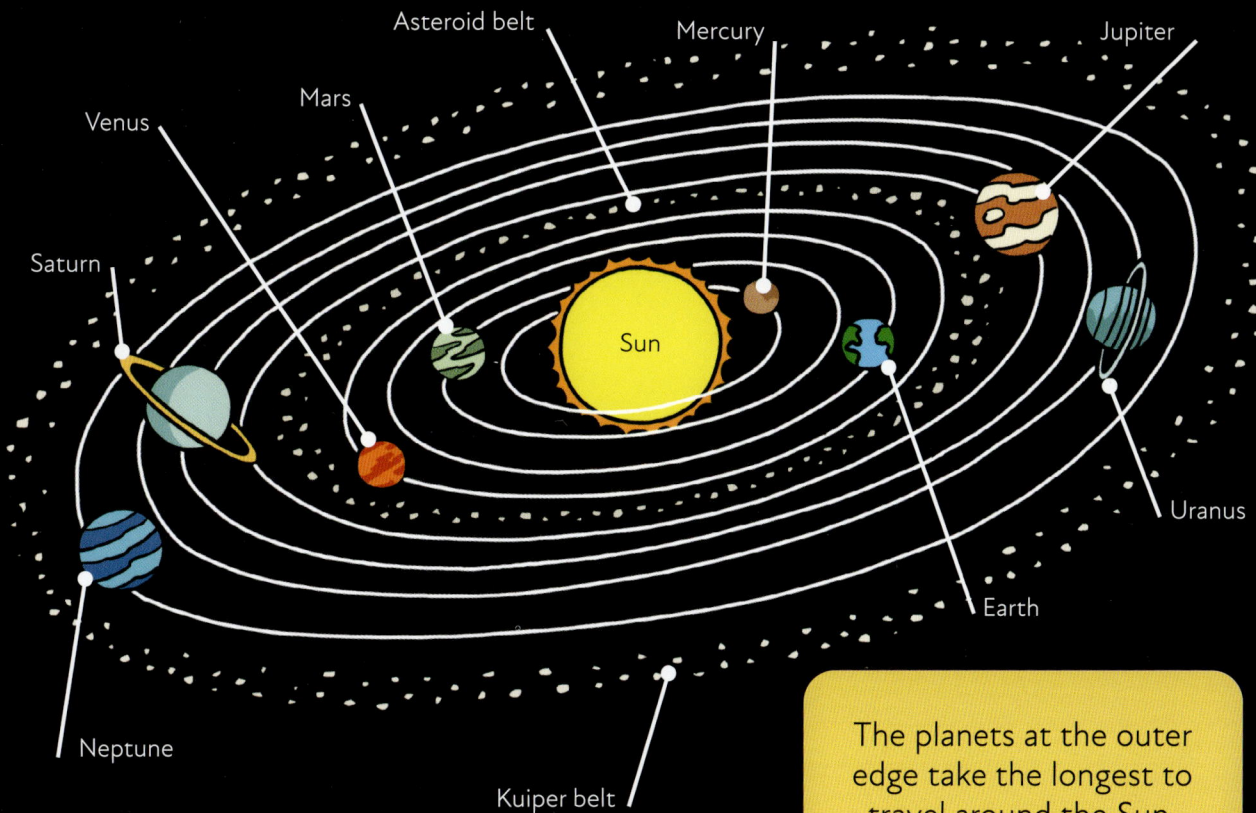

Asteroid belt

Mercury

Jupiter

Mars

Venus

Saturn

Sun

Earth

Uranus

Neptune

Kuiper belt

The planets at the outer edge take the longest to travel around the Sun.

The planets are split into two groups – the inner planets and outer planets. The inner planets are those closest to the Sun: Mercury, Venus, Earth and Mars.

I think I'll take a tour of the whole Solar System! Let's plot a course to the planet closest to the Sun.

Mercury is the smallest planet in the Solar System and the planet closest to the Sun. It can reach blistering temperatures of up to 430°C, dropping to -180°C on the side facing away from the Sun.

It looks a lot like Earth's moon.

Mercury spins around very slowly compared to the Earth, so one day on Mercury is the same as 58 Earth days! But the years are pretty short – it orbits the Sun in just 88 Earth days.

Mercury spins around three times in two orbits (years), so each Mercury day lasts for two Mercury years. This means you'd get to celebrate two birthdays every day!

Happy birthday to me!

Happy birthday to me again!

Venus is the second planet from the Sun. It is almost the same size as Earth but it's a totally different world, covered by over a thousand volcanoes and swirling with hot clouds of poisonous acid and super-fast winds.

Venus is even hotter (464°C) than Mercury, despite being further away from the Sun.

While almost all planets spin anti-clockwise, Venus rotates clockwise. So on Venus, the Sun rises in the west and sets in the east – the opposite of Earth. This direction change is because Venus is upside down!

The last of the inner planets, Mars is known as the red planet because of its red-brown rocks and dust.

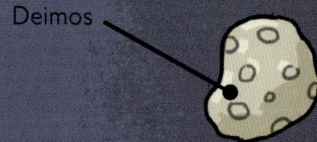

Phobos

Deimos

Ice-covered poles

Mars has two tiny potato-shaped moons, called Phobos and Deimos.

Ingenuity helicopter

Wheeeee!
Wait – what's that?

Mars is filled with gigantic volcanoes and huge canyons. The largest volcano is called Olympus Mons and it's the biggest in the whole Solar System.

Because Mars is the most similar planet to Earth, scientists believe it's one of the best places to search for signs of life.

my class will never believe this!

This chilly, rocky planet has had the most robot visitors. We've sent tough rovers and drones to explore, take pictures, collect soil samples and report their findings to Earth.

Sunsets on Mars look blue because of the way dust particles scatter the light.

The rovers have found signs of liquid water trapped under the rocks, and scientists are now developing technology to send humans to live and study on the red planet.

Next stop: the outer planets! This far away from the Sun, these planets are larger and much colder – and Jupiter is the largest of them all.
You could fit around 1,000 Earths in Jupiter.

Jupiter has 95 moons.
Its largest, Ganymede, is larger than Mercury.

Great Red Spot

Jupiter has the fastest spin of all the planets. One day is just over 10 Earth hours.

Jupiter is covered in swirling bands of gas clouds. The 'Great Red Spot' on its surface is actually a massive storm, twice the size of Earth, and has been raging for over a hundred years.

Saturn is famous for its spectacular rings. There are seven of them (labelled A, B, C, D, E, F and G) and they are made of billions of chunks and particles of ice that reflect the Sun's light.

Saturn doesn't just have rings – it also has a record 146 moons.

While most of the inner planets are rocky, the outer planets are known as the Gas Giants. They might have a small rocky core, but they are mostly made of the gases hydrogen and helium.

Did that last moon hop knock me over, or is this planet wonky?

Uranus gets its hazy blue-green colour from a small amount of methane gas in its atmosphere.

Uranus is a bit topsy-turvy. It's tipped on its side and (like Venus) spins clockwise. As it slowly orbits the Sun, each half of the planet gets sunlight for 42 years, followed by darkness for 42 years. But decades of sunlight can't warm this chilly ice planet, which has an average temperature of -215°C!

Uranus also has rings but they're not as well known as Saturn's. There are 13 of them, mostly faint and dark with two brighter outer rings.

Forget the rings – I read that Uranus's moons are named after Shakespeare characters.

I wouldn't mind a moon named after me ...

The eighth and final planet in this Solar System tour is Neptune.
This icy blue ball takes 165 Earth years to orbit the Sun.

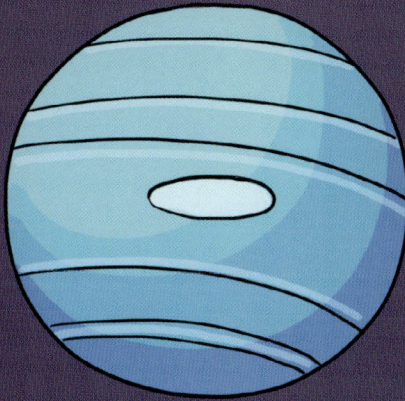

Finally! What a jewel.

Neptune was the first planet to be discovered by maths! An astronomer predicted its existence and location. It took another astronomer just an hour with a telescope and the calculations to find the planet in the night sky and prove the maths was correct.

Voyager 2 is the only spacecraft to have visited Uranus and Neptune as they are so far away. It discovered new rings and moons before carrying on its journey out of the Solar System.

Doesn't my spacecraft count?

So long, Solar System!

The first person to study the night sky through a telescope was the Italian scientist Galileo Galilei, around 1609.

Since then, our telescopes have got bigger and better. The Extremely Large Telescope (ELT) in Chile has a diameter of almost 40 m.

Great snaps! Do you want to see my pics?

We have even launched telescopes into space for a clearer view. The Hubble Telescope was launched in the 1990's, and the James Webb Space Telescope in 2021.

We send spacecraft like probes to planets and moons to get a closer look, take samples and send data to scientists back home.

A probe sent to Jupiter was named Galileo after the astronomer.

The *Parker Solar* probe is on a mission to investigate our own star - the Sun - without getting fried by its heat. It's learning more about the surface of the Sun, as well as things like solar flares and the Sun's magnetic field.

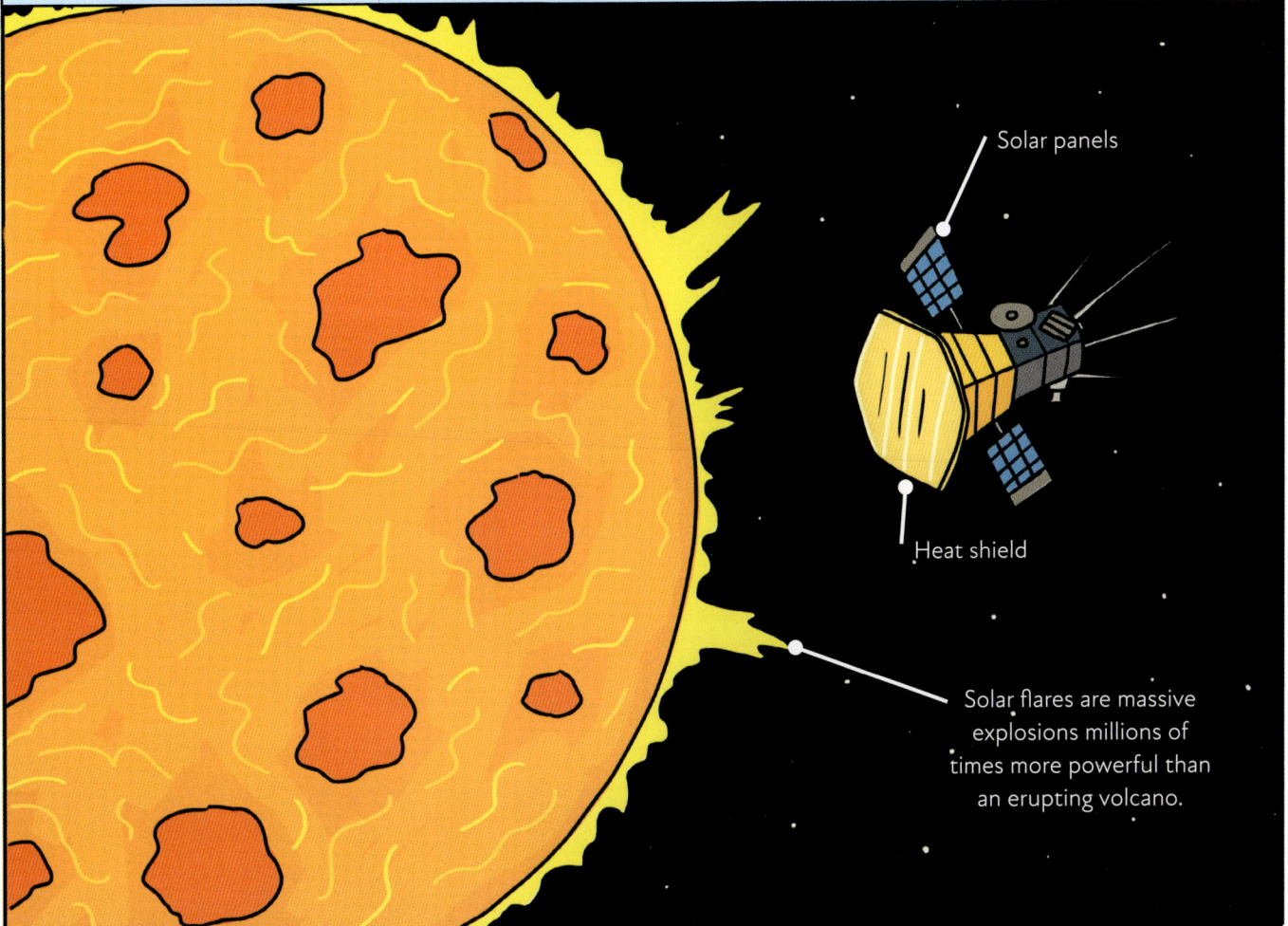

Solar panels

Heat shield

Solar flares are massive explosions millions of times more powerful than an erupting volcano.

We also send probes to smaller objects, such as comets, asteroids and meteoroids.

The *Philae* probe landed on a comet to see what it was made of.

Comets are small lumps of mixed dust, frozen water and other bits and pieces. They have a long, streak-like, glowing tail. Some are unexpected and appear suddenly. Others come back time and again after gaps of years as they orbit the Sun.

Asteroids are rocky lumps, smaller than planets, which orbit the Sun. Most asteroids are found in the wide gap between the planets Mars and Jupiter called the asteroid belt (see page 13).

Uh oh ...

The asteroid that landed on Earth and killed the dinosaurs left a crater over 150 km wide.

A sudden streak of light in the night sky is often called a shooting star, but it's actually a meteoroid burning up in Earth's atmosphere, creating a glowing tail.

Oooo!!

Loads of shooting stars together are called meteor showers and they occur at certain times every year. One of the most well-known showers is called the Perseids; they occur every August.

The *New Horizons* probe is investigating the Kuiper Belt just beyond Neptune (see page 13). The belt is filled with millions of rocky and icy objects, including dwarf planets (not quite big enough to be official planets).

Our Solar System has at least five recognised dwarf planets:
Ceres
Pluto
Haumea
Makemake
Eris

Some consider the Kuiper Belt as marking the edge of our Solar System.

What's next for space exploration? As technology improves, we can expect to look even closer at our Solar System as well as beyond it to galaxies unknown.

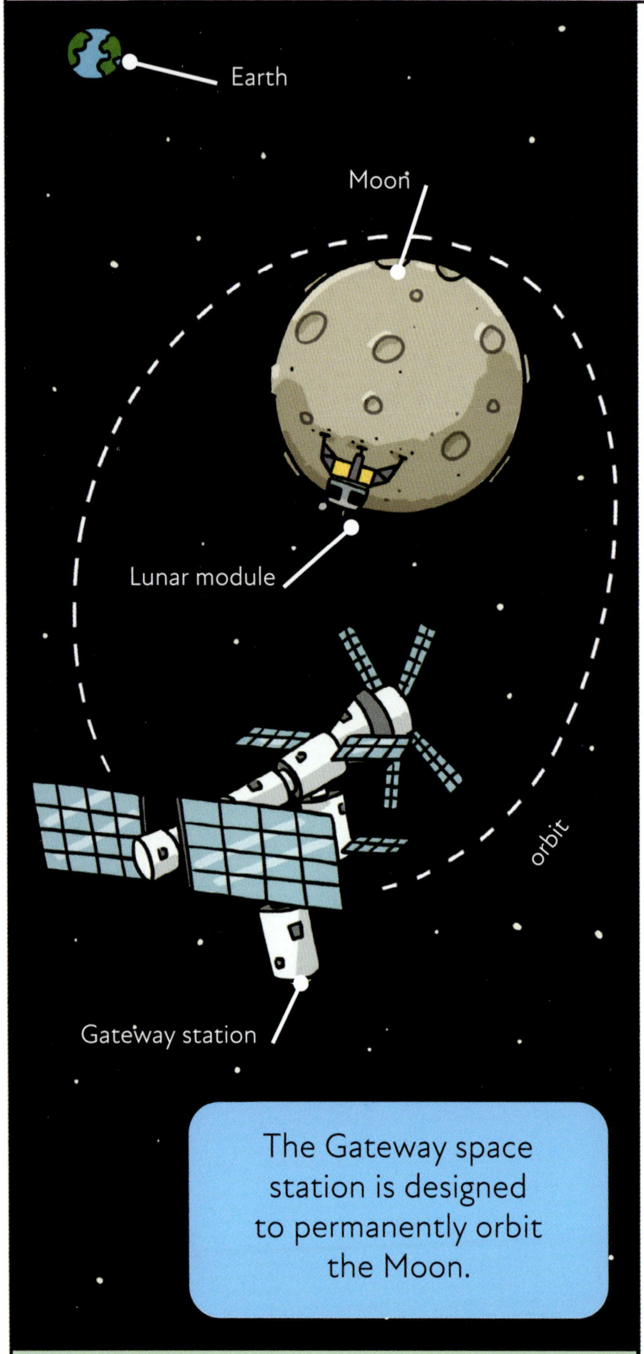
Earth
Moon
Lunar module
orbit
Gateway station
The Gateway space station is designed to permanently orbit the Moon.

First up – we're going back to the Moon! The Artemis missions aim to make the Moon a place to live and work, and a hub from which to explore the rest of the Solar System.

After the Moon, we're hoping to send humans on a two-year journey to Mars and back, but to do this we have to work on new technology.

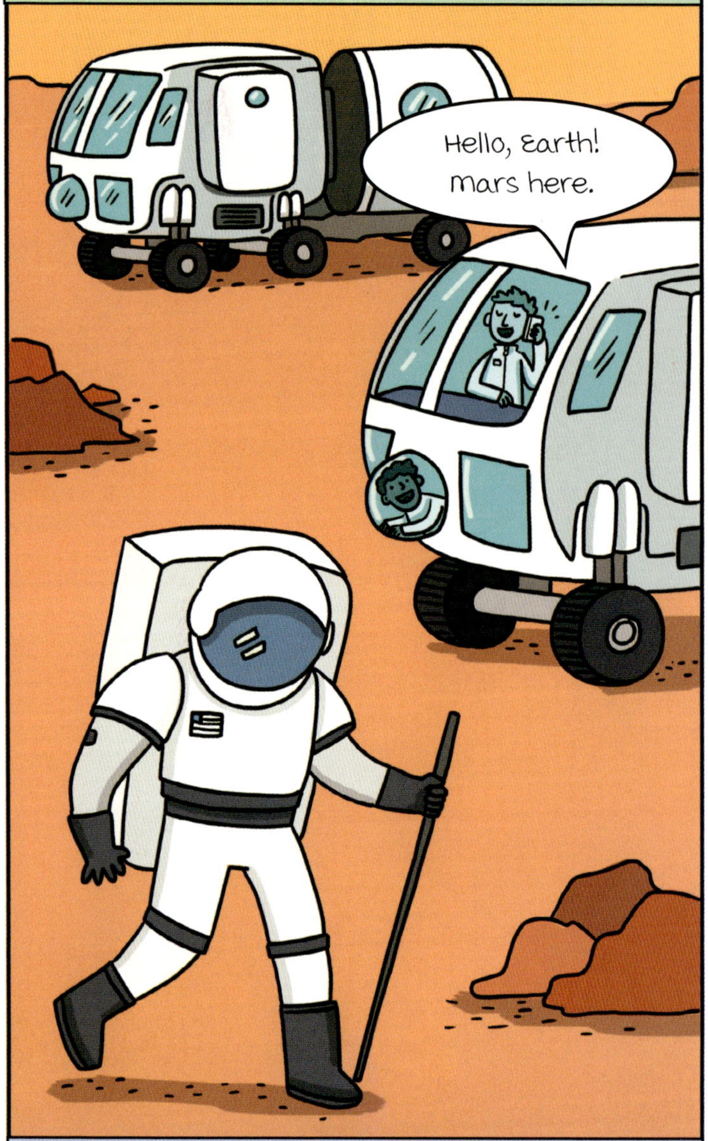
Hello, Earth! Mars here.

This includes new hi-tech spacesuits, homes to live and work in and laser communication systems to stay in touch with Earth.

As well as getting people into space, scientists will still be launching hi-tech probes and robots to gain more and more knowledge about our galaxy and our place within it.

Eight rotors

Dragonfly is designed to fly across Titan, Saturn's largest moon, searching for water and chemicals essential to life.

Cube-shaped robots called Astrobees can fly around a space station, lending astronauts a helping hand.

The Rosalind Franklin rover is the next one to roam the red planet.

More and more people will want to experience travelling to space – for business or for an out-of-this-world holiday – so we can expect space hotels in the future.

It is an incredible view ... It's time to get back down there.

Space is full of wonder, and there is so much still to learn!

maybe we could live on mars!

Are there owls in space?

PROFESSOR HOOT'S SCIENCE SCHOOL

PROFESSOR HOOT'S QUIZ

CAN YOU ANSWER ALL OF PROFESSOR HOOT'S QUESTIONS?

1. How much of Earth is covered by water?
a. 66%
b. 71%
c. 75%

2. When did the first people walk on the Moon?
a. 1969
b. 1970
c. 1975

3. What was the first satellite called?
a. *Sputnik*
b. *Soviet 1*
c. Laika

4. When was the Big Bang?
a. 65 million years ago
b. 13.7 billion years ago
c. 10 billion years ago

5. What is our galaxy called?
a. the Solar System
b. the Universe
c. the Milky Way

6. Which is the hottest planet in the Solar System?
a. Earth
b. Venus
c. Mars

7. Which is the largest planet in the Solar System?
a. Jupiter
b. Saturn
c. Neptune

8. Which planet is furthest from the Sun?
a. Saturn
b. Neptune
c. Uranus

9. How many planets orbit the Sun?
a. 5
b. 8
c. 10

10. Which type of space object hitting Earth led to the dinosaurs dying out?
a. an asteroid
b. a comet
c. a moon

Answers: 1b, 2a, 3a, 4b, 5c, 6b, 7a, 8c, 9b, 10a.

GLOSSARY

astronomer someone who studies the night sky

astronaut a person whose job it is to work and travel in space

atmosphere the layer of gases surrounding a planet

atom the smallest part of an element, from which everything is made

canyon a deep valley in the landscape

clockwise moving in the same direction as the hands of a clock

core the area at the centre of a planet

crater a large hole in the ground

crust the outer layer of a planet

galaxy a huge area of space containing millions of stars, space objects, dust and gas held together by gravity

gravity the force that pulls objects towards each other. On Earth it pulls everything down towards its centre

mantle the part of Earth between the core and the crust

microgravity appearing to have no weight

molecule two or more atoms joined together

moon an object that circles around a planet in space

orbit the path an object follows around another object

particle a very small piece of something

reflect bounce back light or heat

rover a small vehicle that can move around a planet

satellite an object that orbits, or circles around, another object

Solar System the Sun and all the planets, comets and other objects that revolve around it

star a large ball of burning gases in space

telescope a piece of equipment that makes objects that are far away appear closer

Universe everything that exists in space

vegetation trees, grass and other plants

volcano an opening in Earth or another planet's crust that allows hot gases and liquids to escape

PROFESSOR HOOT'S SCIENCE SUGGESTIONS

Check where and when you can spot the International Space Station in the night sky.

https://spotthestation.nasa.gov/

See a close-up view of Mars here:

https://murray-lab.caltech.edu/CTX/V01/SceneView/ MurrayLabCTXmosaic.html

For answers to many questions about space, check out the NASA Spaceplace website.

https://spaceplace.nasa.gov/menu/solar-system/

Read *Recipe for a Solar System* by Professor Raman Prinja (Wayland, 2024)

Want to find out more about each planet in our Solar System?
Read the *Space Station Academy* series by Sally Spray and Mark Ruffle (Wayland, 2024)

Every effort has been made by the Publishers to ensure that the websites in this book are suitable for children, that they are of the highest educational value, and that they contain no inappropriate or offensive material. However, because of the nature of the Internet, it is impossible to guarantee that the contents of these sites will not be altered. We strongly advise that internet access is supervised by a responsible adult.

INDEX